Embracing Hygge Living

Leisure, Hobbies & Lifestyle

Emma Alice Nilsson

Table of Contents

Introduction

"A sense of cozy and comfortable conviviality that engenders a feeling of happiness or well-being, seen as a defining element of Danish culture" is how The Oxford English Dictionary defines hygge (pronounced "hoo-ga"). Although the Danish word cannot be translated precisely into English, it conveys a sense of camaraderie, charm, and comfort in general.

Similar terms include the German gemütlichkeit, the Dutch gezelligheid, and the Swedish mys. Hygge was first popularized in Denmark in the early 1800s. Although the concept of hygge is most prevalent in Denmark, the word comes from the Norwegian word hugga, which is similar to the English word "hug" and roughly means "to comfort."

So where do hobbies fit into hygge? A hobby is an enjoyable interest you engage in during your free time. A hygge hobby, however, goes a step further and defines it as a pastime or activity that not only elicits a feeling of happiness but also relieves stress and anxiety. It is something that helps you become more mindful of the present.

However, if it's something like knitting, it's not just a joy; it also results in a finished item, which adds yet another layer of hygge. Hobbies can include DIY projects, woodworking, carving, knitting, sewing, mindfulness exercises like yoga and tai chi, sports, and even travel.

A hygge pastime can be defined as anything that makes you feel happy and cozy. Simple joys also fulfill many hygge criteria. Simple activities that are very hygge and help us relax and calm down include biking rather than getting in a car, strolling the dog, and taking the family or friends on a ramble around the countryside. Sports and physical activity also play a massive role in our lives.

Even though not everyone needs to engage in physically demanding activities, physical activity is crucial for our health and is an essential component of hygge. Regular walks with family and friends or joining a jogging club, cycling club, ramblers association, or bird watching group improves our quality of life. It helps us enjoy our leisure time while still feeling connected to the community.

Chapter 1: Creating The Hygge Mood At Home

Using Natural Light In Your Space Effectively

We require natural light to be happy and healthy. It heightens our awareness and enhances our mood, productivity, and attitude. It significantly affects our body because it's how we produce vitamin D, which is crucial for a robust immune system and bone density.

There are many approaches.

- To significantly increase the amount of natural light in the house, try replacing heavy voile or lace curtains with sheer panel coverings.
- Repaint the walls in gentle gray, white, or cream to increase the sense of spaciousness.

- Place mirrors and glossy-surfaced furniture in strategic locations to reflect light and return it into the room.

Try some of these tips, and you'll see how a bright, airy environment fosters tranquility.

Get Comfy And Cozy With Soft Furnishings

Nothing is more romantic than curling up on a sofa covered in pillows and a warm blanket or quilt when it's cold outside.

You can get lost in a book, a movie, or a nap while cocooned in a layer of softness. Cover your sofa with merino wool, faux fur, cashmere cushions, throws, and blankets. These lovely textures are ideal for nesting into and instantly add warmth and richness to any space. Put on your coziest jammies and a pair of wool socks to increase the hygge factor.

Introduce Some Nature Into Your Home

Our bodies and minds benefit from nature's calming effects, which also help to create a welcoming environment. There are numerous ways to introduce character indoors. The prominent places to start are indoor plants and freshly cut flowers. They add brightness and beautiful smells to any area.

Pick some flowers from your yard and put them in jam jars for a rustic appearance. You may also gather attractive stones, shells, and driftwood. You can also build table decorations out of bark, leaves, berries, and pine cones that you gathered on a walk in the countryside or along the coast. Pebbles, hand-crafted ceramics, natural wood flooring, and furniture all add cozy, organic textures to a space.

Using natural materials can make it simple to make your house look lovely and linked to the environment outdoors.

Breath In The Fresh Air

Numerous houseplants are excellent air purifiers for homes. They purify your home's air by removing dangerous toxins and contaminants. The following plants are the best-purchased air-filtering plants.

It would be a great idea to keep one of these plants within 100 square feet of your home or apartment:

- Aloe vera.
- Palm bamboo (Dypsis lutescens)
- Boston fern (Nephrolepis exaltata)
- Banana palm (Musa basjoo)
- Barberton daisy (Gerbera jamesonii)
- Broadleaf lady palm (Rhapis excelsa)
- Mandarin evergreen (Aglaonema)
- English ivy (Hedera helix)
- Flamingo lily
- Elephant ear philodendron (Philodendron domesticum)
- Devil's ivy (Epipremnum aureum) (Anthurium andraeanum)
- Flowershop daisy (Chrysanthemum morifolium)
- Lily grass (Liriope muscari)
- Kimberly queen fern (Nephrolepis obliterate)
- Heart-leaf philodendron (Philodendron cordatum);
- Moth orchids (Phalaenopsis)
- Peace lily; (Spathiphyllum)

Enjoying Open Fires

One of life's greatest pleasures is unwinding in front of a fire. Whether in front of an open hearth or a contemporary wood burner, a log fire's crackles and flickering flames produce a warm, inviting ambiance. The soothing scent of wood smoke induces feelings of calmness and contentment, fundamental connection, and a sense of community.

The fireplace serves as the focal point and the center of the house, where tales are told, and occasions are celebrated. Invite loved ones and friends to spend time together around the fire enjoying simple pleasures like roasting marshmallows or playing games, or just relax and take in the beauty of the dancing flames.

Storing And Stacking Firewood

If you have a wood-burning stove or open fireplace, you are likely aware of how crucial it is to have enough logs on hand to get you through the chilly winter months. One of the copious definitions of hygge is enjoying a warm fire while sitting down. But did you know that adequately stacked firewood is essential for a fire to burn efficiently?

How to successfully hasten wood drying

To hasten drying, first purchase logs that have been split into short lengths, ideally 10 inches (25 cm) long. Then keep your logs in a log store that has good ventilation. Many people make the mistake of piling the logs on the ground and covering them with a tarp, but doing so promotes the growth of mold and deterioration. One of the most fundamental elements in keeping your firewood dry is air circulation. Therefore, purchasing a log store will pay off because it enables the wood to be stored above the ground.

It should have a roof over the top and be airy on the sides. Place the log storage on the house's protected side. Your wood should be stacked in rows with spaces between them to promote airflow. Leave about 4 inches (10 cm) between the logs and the surface if stacking against a wall or fence. The most crucial aspect of well-stacked wood is that it will be nice and dry when you need it.

Dry wood burns more successfully and produces less smoke. Note: Dry firewood is never in short supply in a warm, comfortable, hyggelig home!

Setting Up The Table

Setting a lovely table doesn't just have to be for special occasions; you can do it daily to make every meal memorable. It doesn't have to be expensive; paper or linen napkins and a basic white tablecloth, as well as recently-picked flowers in a jam jar, a spray of fall leaves, or a collection of beach treasures arranged in the middle of the table, produce a simple yet attractive outcome.

Glass and candles instantly provide shine and ambiance. When hosting a gathering, don't worry about making everything perfect; a simple spread of cheeses, olives, bread, and wine, or even just some baked buns, will demonstrate the love and care you put into your meal.

Lighting Up The Candles

Danish individuals burn more candles per person than any other Europeans for a good reason: sharing hyggelig moments is crucial while enduring the bleak Scandinavian winters and leaden skies, and lighting candles is one of the easiest methods to create a warm and welcoming atmosphere.

Place lanterns, candles, and tea lights throughout your house—next to your computer, around the fireplace, and on the dining room table—the more sparkling lights, the better. Place your candles cautiously because anything that can start a fire within your house can be harmful. This list of essential dos and don'ts will ensure that you stay safe:

Do:

- You should keep candles out of the path of curtains, fabrics, and other overhanging objects.
- To ensure that candles are held erect and won't tip over, place them in the appropriate holders.

- You should always place candles on a heatproof surface. You should use tea lights with extra caution since they can get hot enough to melt plastic.
- You should always handle candles carefully since they become liquid when lit. Place them on a metal or glass plate.
- Make sure that youngsters and pets cannot get your candles.

Don't Do:

- If you perhaps leave the room, do not leave the candles burning.
- Because clothing and hair can quickly catch fire, never lean over a candle.
- It would help if you didn't place a candle underneath a shelf because it could easily burn the surface's underside.
- Don't blow out a candle when putting it out because doing so can cause hot wax and sparks to fly. To put it out, use a spoon or a snuffer.
- Never let a youngster go to sleep with a burning candle or oil burner in their bedroom.
- Avoid moving a burning candle— always snuff out the flame first.

Different Waxes

Paraffin wax is used to make the majority of candles. A by-product of crude oil, paraffin wax is frequently combined with chemicals to increase burn speed. Many people worry that burning these candles may generate poisonous black soot and other air pollutants. Alternative waxes burn cleaner and produce less smoke and soot.

Although beeswax costs more than paraffin wax, it is a natural wax made by honeybees. Another option is soybean-derived soy wax. It can be made entirely of soybean oil, which is less expensive than beeswax, or you can mix it with other vegetable oils or waxes.

Essential Oils

Purchase candles with essential oil infusions. Essential oils can impact our thoughts, emotions, and moods, improve our well-being, and infuse the space with lovely scents. Different oils have different effects on us. Some essential oils are relaxing, like lavender and bergamot, while others are energizing, like lemon and rose.

If you are perhaps dealing with any of the below adverse health issues, try some of the following:

- Insomnia: lavender, chamomile, jasmine, rose, and sandalwood
- Stress: lavender, bergamot, vetiver, pine, and ylang-ylang
- Anxiety: Roman chamomile, rose, clary sage, lemon, and sandalwood
- Depression: Chamomile, jasmine, peppermint, and chamomile
- Sage, peppermint, and cinnamon can help with memory and concentration issues.
- Clove, jasmine, tea tree, rosemary, sage, and citrus are low-energy plants.

Clothing: Casual Is Key

On Copenhagen's streets, you won't see many three-piece suits, and if you're a member of the pinstriped business set, you'll probably think the Danish dressing method is downright messy. One can say that being informal and elegant at the same time is a Danish art that you might learn to master through time.

Many people, including me, prefer the combination of a T-shirt or sweater on the inside and a jacket on the exterior for a casual yet sophisticated style. For coziness and the professor style, I love the ones with leather patches on the elbows.

My friends tease that if they need to find me when I'm standing with my back to them in a crowded pub, they only need to watch out for the patches, so I may have a slight tendency to misuse the patches.

How To Dress Like A Dane

Danish fashion is streamlined, beautiful, minimalistic, yet not overly fussy. It strikes a balance between minimalist, practical design, and hygge in many ways.

Scarves

A scarf is necessary. Both men and women are subject to this. Despite being mainly used in the winter, people with scarf withdrawal symptoms have been seen using scarves in the middle of summer. The maxim is simple: the bigger, the better. So cover yourself in style with a densely wrapped scarf, but be sure to stop short of causing any neck damage.

Black

You might think that you have just entered the set of a ninja movie as you exit the airport in Copenhagen. In Denmark, black is the dominant color. You want to go for a sleek, monochromatic appearance that would be appropriate for Karl Lagerfeld's funeral. You can choose from a greater variety of hues in the summer, even something outrageously bold like gray.

Top bulky

You can strike a balance between hygge and fashion by wearing hand-knitted wool sweaters, jumpers, cardigans, and pullovers on top, along with black leggings for women and skinny jeans for men. Never wear sloppy sweaters; they can be bulky. Also, don't forget the scarf.

Layers

Layering is the secret to enduring four seasons in one day. Always have an extra cardigan with you. When you're freezing, hygge is impossible.

Woolen socks

As hygge insurance, arm yourself with a beautiful pair of wool socks.

Casual hair

The Danish haircut is so informal that it almost seems lazy. Get up and leave. For girls, a bun is an option; the higher, the better.

Hygge Tip: How To Buy

Connect purchases to satisfying experiences. I had saved up money for a new favorite chair, but I didn't purchase it until after my first book was released. In this sense, the chair serves as a reminder of a significant victory I had.

You can use the same logic for that unique sweater or those lovely wool socks. When you put them on, you want to be reminded of that truly hyggelig moment, so save for them.

Togetherness

Creating cultures and lifestyles that support the development of social interactions is essential. Naturally, concentrating on a healthy work-life balance is one solution. And when it comes to this, many people are envious of Denmark. There is a lot of carefree contemplation when hygge is present.

Nobody monopolizes the talk or seizes the spotlight for protracted periods of time. Because everyone participates in the tasks that make up the hyggelig evening, equality, a quality that is firmly ingrained in Danish society, is a critical component of hygge. Instead of leaving the host alone in the kitchen, it is more hyggelig if we all participate in the meal preparation.

Time spent with others cultivates a pleasant, laid-back, amiable, down-to-earth, close, cozy, and welcoming environment. It resembles a good embrace in many respects, but without physical contact. You can be who you are and be entirely at ease in this circumstance. Therefore, extending your comfort zone to include other individuals is part of the art of hygge.

Oxytocin: What's love got to do with it?

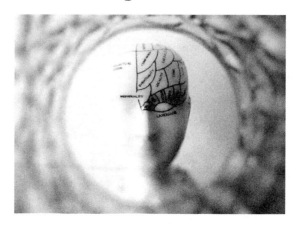

But when do we enjoy having oxytocin circulating through our bodies? Hugs are often believed to make us happier, and this is true—oxytocin begins to flow in close settings, which fosters human connection. As a result, it is also known as "the hormone of affection" or "the hormone of cuddling."

Given that hygge is an intimate activity frequently associated with coziness and some companionship, it stands to reason that oxytocin will be released in these situations. Pet cuddles have the same effect as human cuddles in making us feel cherished, warm, and safe—three of hygge's main components.

Since it fosters collaboration, trust, and love among people, oxytocin—also known as "social glue"—is released when we are physically close to another person's body. Perhaps this explains why Danes have such a high level of trust in total strangers; they practice hygge frequently because hyggelige activities cause the release of oxytocin, which reduces antagonism and fosters social connection.

This hormone is also released by warmth and fullness. Candles, fires, warm blankets, and delectable food go hand in hand with hygge. Hygge is, in a sense, all about oxytocin. Could it be that easy? Maybe it's not a surprise that anything hygge-related makes us feel content, at ease, and secure.

The dark side of hygge

There are undoubtedly advantages to spending time with your close friends in a close-knit social network where you all have a long history together and are well acquainted. However, in recent years I have also come to understand that there is a severe disadvantage to such a social landscape: it is not receptive to newcomers.

I've heard the same thing from every expat I've met who's settled in Denmark. The social circles there are almost impossible to enter. Or, at the very least, it necessitates years and years of diligence and perseverance. Admittedly, Danes struggle to include new people in their social networks.

This is partly because of the idea of hygge; if there were too many unfamiliar faces at an event, it would be deemed less hyggeligt. It takes a lot of work and loneliness along the way to join a social group. The good news is that, in my friend Jon's words, "Once you're in, you're in," You may be confident that once you succeed, you will have made friends for life.

Hygge-socializing for introverts

It is well recognized that introverts get their energy from within, while extroverts get theirs from stimuli outside themselves. Extroverts are the people you should hang out with if you want to have a good time; introverts are frequently perceived as loners. However, social gatherings are not for everyone and may leave an introvert overstimulated and weary.

Social introverts do exist despite the misconception that introversion is synonymous with shyness. (Just as calm extroverts do) This may sound a bit clichéd, but introverts often prefer to devote their "social time" to loved ones whom they know very well, to have meaningful conversations, or to sit down and read a book with something warm to drink. This happens to have a very high hygge factor—significant, right?

Introverts are social but in a different way. There is no single way of being social, but it might feel like there are right and wrong ways. Just because too many external stimuli drain introverts doesn't mean they don't want to hang out with other people. With hygge, introverts may have a lovely, relaxed evening with a few friends without engaging in a lot of activity or chatting with a large group of people.

Hygge, which is an aspect between mingling and relaxing, may be an alternative for introverts who prefer to stay home rather than go to a big party with lots of strangers. It merges these two worlds, which is fantastic for introverts and extroverts because it creates a middle ground.

Therefore, to all of you introverts out there, please do not feel ashamed or uninterested for having a preference for hygge-related items. And to all the extroverts:

- Turn on some soft music.
- Light some candles.
- For the evening, embrace your inner introvert.

Hygge Tip: How to make memories

We all agree that creating memories is the most delicate part of having them. Create a brand-new custom with your loved ones or friends. Two examples are the summer solstice celebration by the water or playing board games on the first Friday of each month. In actuality, it can be any worthwhile activity that, over time, brings the group closer together.

Chapter 2: Decorating Your Home

Hygge is about creating a sense of contentment and happiness; you don't need to spend a fortune to achieve this in your house. Decorate your home with things that make you happy, like fresh flowers. On country treks, you should gather flowers and pine cones. Add items as well. They bring up pleasant memories, like paper snowflakes and seasonal bunting.

These small details make a house feel welcoming. When your visitors are satisfied, you'll know you've done it correctly.

This is to say that they enter through the door with a smile!

Refreshing Flowers

Fresh flowers are the best thing for the heart and soul. Pick aromas that make you smile, like sweet hyacinths or fragrant lilies, and decorate your home with blossoms that make you joyful, such as bold tulips, romantic roses, and colorful daffodils. Hygge is about loving yourself, so go out and treat yourself to a bouquet of your favorite flowers instead of waiting for someone to buy them for you.

Take fresh peonies, lavender, and sweet peas from your window box or garden. You can use jugs, jam jars, glass bottles, Mason jars, and even mugs if you don't have enough vases. The flowers should be placed where you can see them daily, whether in a bouquet or just one eye-catching stem.

Creating A Natural Display

Do your pockets usually include strange stones, twigs, and plant material when you get home from a walk? Finding it difficult to decide what to do with all of them? If you make any discoveries, create a nature display when you get home. Have fun gathering your items and thinking of inventive ways to showcase them.

You may even put together a display using beach driftwood and shells or fill glass jars with unusual rocks and pebbles collected from the seaside. When arranged in sizable vases or bowls, Berry branches and pine cones make a statement. These branches are large enough to be used as hanging mobiles from the ceiling. Limit your display to more than a little table in the corner.

Try arranging your treasures in a box or tray, or display them prominently on a mantelpiece or shelf. This is a beautiful way to reconnect with nature's wonders, and the best part is that the whole family can take part. Happy gathering!

Things to collect

- Moss, pine cones, hazelnuts, twigs, fallen tree bark, chestnuts, sycamore helicopters, and acorns can be found in the countryside and the woods.
- Sunflower seed pods, dried sunflower seeds, dandelion clocks, stones, leaves, flowers, squash, and gourds are all found in gardens.

- Shells (without organisms inside), dried seaweed, seagull feathers, mermaid purses, and shark teeth can all be found on the beach.

Paper Snowflakes

By creating these paper snowflakes, you can grant your wishes for a snowy day. They're easy to make and make your house look like a winter wonderland. You can hang them from the ceiling, string them together to create a garland, or affix them to windows to create a customized snow scene.

Making paper snowflakes will instantly take you back to your childhood Christmases when they were full of enchantment and wonder.

What you'll need

- White square paper (lightweight craft paper works best)
- Scalpel or razor-sharp scissors

Instructions

1. Take one square of paper. To create a triangle, fold the paper in half diagonally.
2. The triangle should be folded twice, with the two sharp edges aligned. Proceed to fold the triangle into thirds (make sure the sides match up).
3. Cutting straight across the triangle's shortest edge eliminates the triangle's two bottom points.

4. Trim away shapes from the folded paper's edges. You should carefully open the paper to display your creation.

Carving pumpkins

The end of October signals one thing: it's time to dress in frightening attire and carve pumpkins into lanterns! An enjoyable social activity for family and friends is pumpkin carving. The best part? A lit candle within the pumpkin will give a lovely, comforting glow that will scare away witches and werewolves.

Instructions on how to carve a pumpkin

Use a sharp knife to cut off the pumpkin's stem at the top since it's more challenging than you might imagine.

Remove the flesh and seeds with a spoon; kids enjoy this messy step. Save the seeds for future planting.

Use a felt-tip pen to draw or sketch a face or other design onto the pumpkin. You should use a sharp knife to cut out the patterns.

Insert some natural or artificial tea lights into the pumpkin. Place the stem back on like a lid after lighting them.

Place your carved pumpkin outside on the doormat, a windowsill, or a gatepost to enchant guests and onlookers and brighten a gloomy, chilly evening.

Bunting In The Winter

Homemade bunting is a quick and enjoyable way to add a festive atmosphere to any indoor space. It gives a room a lovely border and a hint of charming rusticity. It's simple to make, and you can use scraps of paper, pieces of fabric, old clothing, and even plastic and paper bags to build your bunting. Have a relaxing craft day at home and let your creativity run wild.

What you'll need

- Cardboard (Thin)
- Attractive textiles and materials
- Glue or thread and needle
- String, twine, or ribbon
- To hang the bunting, use drawing pins (optional)
- Scissors

Instructions

1. Create a cardboard triangle template.
2. Cut numerous triangles using the template from the material of your choice (winter)—Tartan (for example)
3. Designs like snowflakes, icicles, and pine trees, as well as warm colors, work well.
4. Attach the triangles to a piece of ribbon, thread, or natural twine using glue or stitching.

5. Deciding where to hang your bunting is the most challenging step in the procedure! It enhances the design of bedrooms and gives kitchens and living spaces a unique touch. As long as it isn't too close to the fire, you can hang it on walls, fasten it to shelves, or use it as a garland for a mantelpiece.
6. Once your bunting is up, bring some friends to check it out (this is the ideal pretext for a night of board games, beverages, and snacks!).

Your Hygge Headquarters

Because our homes serve as the center of hygge, the Danes are obsessed with interior design. In Denmark, social life revolves around the house. The social life of other nations typically takes place in bars, restaurants, and cafés, but the Danes prefer hjemme hygge (home hygge), among other things, because they don't like paying the high rates in restaurants.

According to a study, seven out of ten Danes feel the most at home 'at home'. The Kähler Vase Scandal, also known as Vasegate, is arguably the clearest example of the Danish concern with design. The Kähler vase was a limited edition anniversary item that went on sale on August 25, 2014.

On that particular day, more than 16,000 Danes attempted to purchase it online, most in vain since the vase immediately sold out. Long lineups of customers formed outside the retailers stocking the vase after the website failed. The limited supply caused a public outcry against the firm that made the vase.

Hygge wishlist

- Cushions and blankets
- Vintage
- Think Tactile
- Ceramics
- Books

- Nature
- Things made out of wood
- Candles
- A Fireplace
- A Hyggerkrog

Blankets and cushions

Any hygge home needs to include blankets and pillows, especially during the chilly winter months. It's highly hyggeligt to cuddle up with a blanket, and occasionally people do it even when they are not cold since it is cozier. Fabrics like wool or fleece, which are warmer, or cotton, which feels lighter, can be used to make blankets.

Cushions of all sizes are needed for hygge. What could be more comforting than reading your favorite book while resting your head on a comfortable pillow? You are free to go Freudian on the Danes at this point and observe that hygge appears to be focused on comfort food and cozy blankets.

Vintage

Antique or retro stores are great places to uncover vintage items. It can be challenging to spot diamonds amid a sea of coal. A truly hyggeligt lamp, table, or chair has seen better days. In a vintage shop, one can find everything they need to furnish a beautiful home, and the items inside are made all the more exciting and cozier by their history.

Many of these goods play on tales and nostalgia. Objects have emotional worth and history in addition to their physical characteristics.

Think tactile

Your hyggelig interior is not just about how things seem, as you may have already realized, but also how they feel. It feels very different to touch anything made of steel, glass, or plastic than it does to run your fingers across a hardwood table, over a warm ceramic cup, or through the hairs of a reindeer's skin. Add a range of textures to your home and consider how things feel to the touch.

Ceramics

They are all attractive, whether a gorgeous teapot, a vase on the dining room table, or your go-to mug. Two of the most famous Danish ceramic brands are Kähler, which has a history dating back more than 175 years.

It made a significant impression at the Universal Exposition in Paris in 1889—the year the Eiffel Tower was inaugurated—and Royal Copenhagen, established in 1775 under the patronage of Queen Juliane Marie. This has recently experienced a resurgence in popularity thanks to the Blue Fluted Mega range.

Books

Who doesn't enjoy a shelf stacked high with weighty books? One of the pillars of the hygge philosophy is unwinding with a good book. No matter the genre, romance, science fiction, cooking manuals, or even horror stories are welcome on the shelves.

Every book is cozy, but great works by writers like Jane Austen, Charlotte Bronte, Leo Tolstoy, and Charles Dickens have a unique place in the library. When they're old enough, your children might also enjoy reading aloud to them when they're curled up next to you in the hyggekrog.

Nature

Wood is insufficient. The entire forest must be brought indoors for the Danes. Any bit of nature you come upon is going to be considered hygge. Animal skins, twigs, leaves, nuts, and flowers. Essentially, you should think: How would a Viking squirrel decorate a living room?

To add even more hygge, cover those window sills, benches, and chairs in sheepskin. Sheep and reindeer may be alternated, while cowhide is reserved for the floor. Copenhagen has been burned to the ground multiple times, which is not surprising given the Danes' penchant for candles, wood, and other flammable materials.

Things made out of wood

There is something about wooden objects that may be a hankering for our origins. The smooth feel of a wooden bureau, the quiet creak of a hardwood floor as you stumble across it to take a seat in the wooden chair by the window, the smell of burning wood from a fireplace, or even a match.

After years of plastic toys, wooden children's toys are now in demand. An excellent illustration of this is the wooden monkey by Kay Bojesen. Wood brings us closer to nature since it is uncomplicated and organic, just like the hygge aesthetic.

Candles

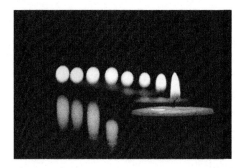

No candles, no hygge, it's just as simple as that. Why may you be wondering? This is because hygge is centered around creating a warm and cozy atmosphere that can be easily attained by having a few candlelights lit.

Fireplace

I had a lucky childhood. The house I happened to grow up in had a wood-burning stove and an open fireplace. My favorite childhood duty was to stack the wood and start the fire. I don't think I'm the only one, though. There are 28 million homes in the country. What motivates the Danish culture's preoccupation with burning wood, then?

I'm sure you already know the answer to this one, but it couldn't only be about hygge, could it?. It is reasonable to say that a fireplace may be the ultimate hygge headquarters. It's a place where we spend time with our loved ones to deepen our sense of community and where we sit by ourselves to rest while experiencing the ultimate sentiments of comfort and warmth.

A Hyggekrog

The one thing every house must have is a hyggekrog, which is Danish for "a nook." It's the room area where you choose to curl up with a book, a cup of tea, and a blanket. Mine is by the window in the kitchen. There are several pillows, a blanket, and a hide from a reindeer there, and I also use it as a workspace at night.

Indeed, a large portion of these pages was written there. Danes adore their cozy surroundings. Hyggekrog is popular in Copenhagen and around the nation, and everyone wants one. As you stroll through the city, you'll see that many structures feature bay windows.

The inhabitants will have a comfortable spot to sit and unwind after a hard day in these interior spaces, which are almost certainly equipped with pillows and blankets. However, even if it is hyggeligt, you don't have to have your hyggekrog there. It may be a section of a room.

You may create your hyggekrog in your home, where you can unwind with a good book and something to drink, by adding cushions or other comfortable items to sit on, soft lighting, and possibly a blanket. In Denmark, creating hyggeligt is a big issue. To sell homes, some real estate brokers even utilize hyggekrog.

Chapter 3: Items That You Can Craft For Instant Hygge

Making something from scratch with your hands is among life's most gratifying joys. Whether you're making a fluffy pair of slippers or a lovely wooly cap with a pom-pom. Anything done by hand exudes personality and originality. The subsequent pages demonstrate how to create comfy accessories and thoughtful gifts that make you feel cozy and content.

Fairy-light lanterns

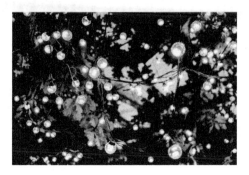

Make some fairy-light lanterns to bring some glimmer into your life. Using fairy lights is a wonderful way to set a distinctive mood. They give off a dreamy, whimsical glow and give every space a hint of charm. Making these lanterns only takes a few minutes, offering a beautiful backdrop for a celebration or a nice night in.

What you'll need

- 1 to 3 big Mason jars
- 1-3 strings of LED fairy lights powered by batteries
- One piece large enough to cover the battery pack of sticky burlap tape

Instructions

1. Use a scrap of burlap to cover the battery pack in one string of fairy lights. Make sure the on/off button is facing up so you can quickly reach in and turn the lights off before carefully placing the battery pack into the bottom of a mason jar.
2. Distribute the fairy lights throughout the jar to cover the interior. (If you're using a particularly large jar, you might need to use multiple strings of fairy lights.)
3. Tape the light string's top to the inside of the lid and then screw the jar's cap back on.
4. You can choose to add a red ribbon to the jar or leave it simple for a more natural appearance.

5. Set the mason jar(s) on a tray or mantelpiece and decorate the base with pine cones, decorations, and confetti stars.
6. Take a step back and admire your creation.

Note: *An alternative is to purchase a string of fairy lights with a battery pack that fits snugly enough to be taped to the jar lid. To conceal the battery pack, affix a thick piece of cloth or ribbon to the jar's neck.*

Mug cozy

Make your favorite mug a savvy little jacket for winter—not only will it look very fetching, but it will also keep your hot chocolate steaming a little bit longer. It's also a genius way to upcycle a wooly sock!

What you'll need

- Ruler
- Mug
- Wooly socks
- Needle and thread
- Scissors
- Fabric glue (Optional)
- Button felt shapes, mini-pom-poms, and sequins are optional embellishments

Instructions

1. Select your preferred cup and gauge its height.
2. Keep the top portion of the sock and cut it off at the ankle.
3. You should turn the top of the sock inside out and use the thread to hem the seams firmly.
4. Cut a slit for the cup handle after turning the sock inside out.
5. To stop the edges from fraying, either overstitch them or apply fabric glue. If using glue, use only a tiny amount so it will dry clear, and let it dry for the amount of time recommended on the bottle. Fit your cozy over the cup after that.
6. By adding creative flourishes using buttons, felt, or anything else your creativity allows, you may give your cup cozy a little additional hygge. Why stop there, then? To prevent your flask from feeling left out, create a comfortable for it similarly.

Pom-Pom for a Beanie Hat

Repurpose one of your worn-out wool hats with some hygge spirit! Making pom-poms is fun, but why stop at one when you can make ten of them in various colors? You and the whole family can do this activity. You can even invite some friends along too.

What you'll need

- Needle and thread
- Yarn

- Scissors
- Cardboard

Instructions

1. To make a larger pom-pom, cut out two cardboard discs that are the same size.
2. Each disc should have a small hole drilled through the center before being stacked. Make that the yarn can fit through the opening.
3. Holding the yarn in place with your fingers at first to prevent it from unraveling, loop it through the holes and around the outside edges of the discs.
4. Continue until the discs are wholly and evenly covered. Cut through the yarn that surrounds the outside edge of the cardboard discs by inserting the scissors between the two cardboard discs.
5. To assemble your pom-pom, carefully wrap a length of thread around the yarn in the space between the two discs, making sure to secure a knot at the end. (Leave enough thread to attach the pom-pom to your hat.)
6. Cut the cardboard and remove it from the pom-pom once the yarn has firmly secured.
7. To make your pom-pom precisely round, fluff it up and, if required, trim it with scissors.
8. Put the pom-pom on your hat and stride into the brisk, chilly air with a cheery bounce.

Note: *Use a variety of colorful yarns to create a pom-pom that is rainbow-hued. You could also purchase self-striping yarn, which will perform all the work for you and give your pom-pom a brighter appearance.*

Felt slippers

The footwear of choice for pajama days must be slippers. No slippers? No issue!

These felt slippers will keep your feet warm all year long. Show your feet some love.

You can even give these to a friend or family member.

What you'll need

- 19.5 x 19.5 inch (50 x 50 cm) Felted wool square
- Scissors
- Chalk for dressmakers or fabric markers
- strong thread made of polyester or silk
- Darning needle, large
- Paper

Instructions

1. Use a photocopier to expand the template below so that it is twice as big and roughly an inch longer than the sole of your shoe before cutting it out.

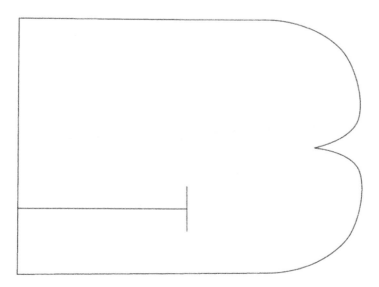

2. Trace the template onto your felt, ensuring that you cut out the T shape with care.

3. Sew the toe seam after folding the felt in half lengthwise. You should pinch the heel seams together. Sew from the top of the slipper to about 2 centimeters (3.5 inches) from the heel. Carefully snip into the heel to form a small flap.

4. This flap should be securely stitched in place. Afterward, flip the slipper inside out and use your scissors to round the flap's edges for a finished look. You have two options: stop there or fold the sides to the ankle and sew them to the slipper. Remember to flip the template, so the T is on the opposite side while sewing the other slipper.

Note: *The possibilities are endless when it comes to adding extra hygge. Consider adding lace, homemade felt flowers, pom-poms, or matching them to your favorite pajamas.*

Lavender bags

Since ancient times, people have utilized lavender for its therapeutic benefits. Its aroma is calming and rejuvenating. Making lavender bags is simple, and they have a variety of uses. Put one under your pillow to promote a restful night's sleep, or stash one in a drawer or wardrobe to keep your clothes and bedding smelling fresh.

When you're having a hectic day, you may even carry one in your handbag or pocket to help you unwind with its delicate perfume.

What you'll need

- Scissors
- Pins
- Pretty fabric (Your choice)
- Dried lavender
- Needle and thread
- Ribbon (Optional)

Instructions

1. Measure the fabric and cut out two rectangles that are 6 by 4.5 inches (16 x 11.5 cm).
2. With the patterned sides facing one another, pin the two rectangles together.

3. Sew around the rectangle, stopping about 34 inches (2 cm) from the other corner, beginning halfway down one of the short sides.

4. You can use the end of a pencil or a paintbrush to push out the corners, so they are pointed before cutting off the corners and turning the rectangle the proper way around while pushing the fabric through the opening you've created.

5. To make the seam across the opening nice and straight, iron it.

6. Fill with dried lavender (available online or from a nearby lavender farm); if you have access to a lavender bush, dry your own.

Note: *Place a loop of ribbon halfway across the top border of the gap if you want to hang your bag up. Then, sew across the gap, backstitching over the ribbon to keep it in place.*

Chapter 4: Seasonal Outdoor/ Indoor Activities/Hobbies

Hygge is more than just staying warm by the fire and blocking out the cold. Whatever the weather, this chapter offers suggestions for getting the most out of nature and bonding with it by utilizing indoor and outdoor activities or hobbies.

Natural Wonders

When It comes to Hygge and natural wonders, there are many activities, hobbies, and practices that one can do to achieve a sense of enrichment. Doing so allows us to get in touch with nature and our surroundings. This is great for experiencing the Hyggelig feeling.

Watching the sunset

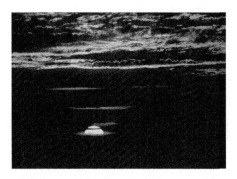

Sunsets have a mystical and innately strong quality. These natural marvels have moved poets and authors for millennia. We should all take the time to appreciate sunsets. Find a location with a view of the western horizon on a clear day. Prepare for the experience by dressing warmly and getting there early.

As the sun descends lower in the sky, pink, orange, and gold hues begin to shimmer. Sit with a friend or a loved one and watch in delight. Regularly engaging in this mindful activity or hobby is a simple way to add more wonder and beauty to your day.

Stargazing

The best time to discover the marvels of the night sky is on a clear night.

A star map and a pair of binoculars are all you need to see some amazing celestial objects. For assistance in navigating the night sky, get an evening sky map from the Internet and buy or borrow a compass.

The ideal place for stargazing is far from towns and other light-polluted areas; consider going to a park, a hill, or a beach. Find the North Star and stars in the Big Dipper, Orion, and Cassiopeia constellations. Watch out for meteors and far-off planets as well. To keep both adults and children happy when stargazing, bring a blanket to lay on, lots of warm clothing, and a flask of hot beverage. Perhaps even a few small eats too.

Bonfires

The ultimate outdoor hyggelig activity is building a bonfire. Organize a gathering with friends and cook over a campfire. Serve potatoes with butter after wrapping them in foil and burying them in the embers until the insides are fluffy and mushy.

Make bonfire bananas, which are roasted bananas that have been cut in half lengthwise and filled with chocolate chips, or roast marshmallows on long sticks for dessert. As you gather around a roaring fire, take a moment to relax and savor the sensation of total comfort and contentment.

How to build a bonfire

- Locate a safe spot away from buildings, fences, trees, shrubs, and garbage or yard waste.
- Create a small pit to put out the flames. It should be about 1 yard (1 meter) broader than you would like your fire to be and about 4 inches (10 cm) deep.
- To keep the fire contained, surround the pit's edge with bricks or big stones.
- Place a tinder bundle (wood shavings, newspaper, twigs, bark, grass, dry leaves, or even moss) on top of the firelighters in the center of the pit.
- To create a tepee shape, arrange the dry kindling atop the tinder at 45-degree angles, meeting in the center so that the

tinder may receive oxygen and leave small spaces in the kindling.

- Drop a lighted match inside the tepee or place it beneath the tinder.
- When the kindling tepee collapses, add logs to feed the fire.
- The tinder should ignite first, then the kindling.
- Make sure you completely extinguish the fire at night's end. Give yourself at least 20 minutes for this because it takes longer than you anticipate. When the fire is cool, dump some dirt or sand on top and spray water over it to extinguish the embers.
- Keep kids away from the fire unless an adult is watching them.

Toasting marshmallows in front of the fire

Nothing is more hyggelig than toasted marshmallows, which are crisp on the exterior and wonderfully mushy on the inside. Place a couple of marshmallows on the end of a kebab stick and sit by your fireplace or fire pit to roast them until they turn golden to relive your childhood.

You can sandwich the marshmallow between two graham crackers, or you can eat it whole. Keep damp wipes on hand for any sticky fingers, and be careful because the deliciousness will be heated inside!

(A simple hyggelig activity you can do with friends and family; that when repeated enough can turn into a unique hobby.)

Fun In The Snow

Modest joys like waking up to the first frost of the year or, even better, the first snowfall are examples of small moments of Hygge. Casting the curtains reveals a world covered with glistening, crystalline snow, which is simply stunning. The only sound in the scene is the crunch of snow underfoot.

Long periods of silence before the action starts! Snow is an excellent justification for acting silly and being a kid once more, having snowball battles, making snowmen, going sledding, and making snow angels. When the joyous shrieks and laughter have subsided, take the whole family for a stroll while you see how the surroundings have converted into a winter wonderland sparkling with snow and ice.

Once you have done this and you have red cheeks and broad smiles, return home where you may enjoy hot drinks by the fire, a family movie, and a head full of fond memories.

Woodland Walks

Wrap up, put on your walking boots, and go to the woods to reconnect with the essential things in life. Woods are excellent locations to look and listen for wildlife since trees provide shelter for various species. You might hear an owl or cuckoo calling, observe fox or badger tracks, or both.

You might even perhaps stumble upon a carpet of bluebells in the spring or discover dazzling conkers dispersed beneath the horse chestnut tree's branches in the fall. It's fun to explore the woods. There are so many items to pick up and gather during the trip, including pine cones, leaves, acorns, and feathers, that you could turn them into a scavenger hunt.

Hug a tree or balance on logs to embrace your playful side. It's a terrific approach to revitalize yourself by spending time in the woods. Trees give forth chemicals and aromas that improve our mood and help us unwind. Go to the woods and take in the calming environment. Who knows, you may just have found your new favorite hobby.

Bike Rides

Few things give you a sense of independence, like riding a bike. It's a fantastic low-impact fitness method that will excite you as you freewheel down hills and bike along tracks, much like you did when you were a kid. Enjoy the relaxing warmth of the sun on your face and the breeze ruffling your hair.

While driving the pedals, stay in touch with your body. There isn't a more enjoyable way to travel in my opinion! And who knows, you may have just found a new healthy hobby.

Picnics

Summer is the season most often associated with picnics. Still, summer also has its drawbacks, such as crunchy sand in your sandwiches, having to shoo curious animals away, and having to flee when an ominous little gray cloud turns into a biblical downpour.

So why not try a picnic in the fall or winter when the weather is brighter? Food unites people, and no setting does it better than a picnic. A pleasant hyggelig experience is to share food and chat while sitting on a blanket. Why not plan a picnic where each person brings a dish to share?

Spread out a lot of blankets in a picturesque location, like a beach, park, forest, or nature reserve; bring additional clothing in case it gets cool. Allow everyone to assist themselves with excellent cuisine on plates, then take a seat and unwind. Picnics can also be spontaneous events. You can take your dinner to the beach, enjoy your lunch in the park, or pack some soup and go on a road trip.

Enjoying the scenery, food, and company of others makes a picnic unique, regardless of where you are or with whom. What's more, you can turn picnicking into your own personal hobby; all you need is repetition.

Note: *Keep in mind that a picnic doesn't have to be challenging to be enjoyable. With hot soup, chili, or stew in a flask, baked potatoes in foil, and hot chocolate and cookies for dessert, keep things straightforward but cozy. Eating outdoors always improves the taste of food!*

Fruit Picking In The Hedgerows

Hedgerows in the autumn are bursting with mouthwatering edible treasure; fruits like elderberries and blackberries are begging to be picked. So gather the untamed hedgerows in a bag or basket.

The entire family can bond with nature while taking advantage of the rest of the pleasant weather by going foraging. Pick mature elderberries in bunches to produce a delightful sweet jelly, or gather sloes to make gin in some areas—pluck blackberries from bushes to make a fruit crumble.

Always check to see if the goods you have foraged are safe to eat, so make sure to bring a guidebook or an expert. However, if you spend a lot of time doing this, it is better to call it what it is—a hobby.

Winter Beach Walks

Winter coastal weather can bring strong winds, rough seas, and bitterly cold temperatures. Still, it also makes the seashore an exciting location for walking, playing games, beachcombing, or simply enjoying being outside in the fresh air. Take a flask of something warm and wrap up against the cold.

Winter is one of the finest seasons for beachcombing because of the intriguing flotsam and jetsam that winter storms produce. At low tide, stroll down and search the shingle for sharks' teeth. You may also bring a kite, ball, and bat and make the most of the ample space to indulge in an array of other activities or enjoy one of your favorite hobbies.

Before leaving

- Check the tide times, especially if you intend to visit a section of the coast that is inaccessible at high tide.
- Wear shoes with grips to prevent slipping on wet rocks or loose shingles.
- Additionally, bring a pair of binoculars in case you happen to notice some coastal birds or a gray seal bobbing in the water.

Chapter 5: Simple Pleasures

Hygge is about appreciating the small things in life and taking the time to enjoy one's company or some well-earned "me time." For a daily dose of Hygge, take some time to indulge in these small pleasures and incorporate them into your life.

A Delightful Candle-lit Bath

One of the quickest methods to enter a delightful state of relaxation and leisure is to take a warm bath. Here's how to make your bathroom a soothing and healing spa retreat. Run your bath while adding a few bath salts to assist your muscles.

Add a couple of drops of one of your favorite relaxing essential oils, such as lavender, neroli, or rose, to the water before entering. Apply a face mask prepared from one mashed banana combined with a tablespoon of orange juice and a spoonful of honey to nourish your skin.

Although it smells delicious enough to eat, resist the urge! The steam will then curl about you while you relax. Candles will add to the coziness. Step out of the bath, rinse your face with warm water, and moisturize after soaking for around 20 minutes.

Put on your coziest bathrobe, relax with a book or a cup of herbal tea, and enjoy a well-earned snooze!

(It's preferable to combine the oil with some olive oil first; adding essential oils directly to hot water causes them to evaporate, quickly reducing therapeutic advantages.)

Reading By The Fireplace

What could be more leisurely than reading an excellent book in front of a roaring fire while listening to the rain patter on the window? Spend some time reading a ghost story, enjoying a thriller, or rereading some old favorites.

Try reading aloud to a special someone while the fire flickers softly in the background. It's the ideal leisure activity to engage in on a gloomy, chilly day or a gloomy winter evening.

Partake In A Feel-Good Movie

Watching a feel-good movie while curled under a blanket or duvet is one of the easiest ways to improve your mood. The following films are sure to make your day better, whether you watch them by yourself or with your family on the couch while holding popcorn and beverages.

Top ten feel-good movies: (My Opinion)

1. Forrest Gump
2. Ferris Bueller's Day Off
3. Back To The Future
4. The Shawshank Redemption
5. Amélie
6. Little Miss Sunshine
7. Dirty Dancing
8. Groundhog Day
9. It's A Wonderful Life
10. Pretty Women

Top ten family films: (My Opinion)

1. Any classic Walt Disney film (e.g., Cinderella, Snow White and the seven dwarfs, Pinocchio)
2. Wallace & Gromit: The Curse Of The Were-Rabbit
3. Beauty and the Beast
4. Toy Story
5. E.T. The Extra-Terrestrial
6. The Goonies
7. Up
8. Shrek
9. Frozen
10. Ratatouille

Playing Games With Family And Friends

Find your favorite leisure board games in the attic and give them a good cleaning. Playing games with your loved ones by the fire may make even the most miserable day enjoyable. Pass out pieces of handmade cake, mulled wine, and freshly brewed coffee.

Connecting with the people in your life while having fun is the primary goal of hyggelig game-playing. Try your hand at a classic game like Jenga or Scrabble to see how agile you are physically and mentally.

Hygge Playlist

The sound of burning wood, the patter of rain on glass, and the crisp flick of pages moving all have a lot to recommend, but these are not the only sounds that convey Hygge. Searching through your music library won't take long to find songs that can help you explore the Scandinavian idea.

Some tunes represent the chill of the outside air, the hug of a loved one, and nights of introspective peace and satisfaction. You can find a hyggelig track on many of your favorite albums, whether it be blues and country, indie, jazz, soul, or whatever genre lights your hygge flame.

You can use your hygge playlist as the ideal background music for various pursuits, activities, or hobbies, or you can just lean back, close your eyes, and drift on the melodic eddies while you enjoy some much-needed leisure time.

Company

Self-hygge is possible. Hyggeligt includes various activities, such as cuddling up under a blanket with your favorite TV show on a rainy Sunday afternoon, sipping red wine while watching a rainstorm, or simply sitting by the window and taking in the scenery.

However, the most humorous times always appear to be shared with others. My father and his two brothers recently celebrated their 50th birthdays, so they hired a sizable summer cabin on Denmark's west coast and invited everyone. Sand dunes surrounded the cabin, which was located in a rugged, barren region where the wind always blows brutally.

There, we did nothing but eat, drink, chat, and stroll down the beach for a whole weekend. That was, in my opinion, the coziest and most leisurely weekend I had that year.

Casualness

The majority of hyggelige moments appear to be constructed on a foundation of leisure or laxness. You must be at ease in order for you and your visitors to Hygge. There is no need to formalize anything. Come as you are and act accordingly.

For instance, I participated in a Champagne grape harvest one fall. I visited the area a few years ago with three friends, and we decided to visit the Marquette vineyard, where I had previously worked. A hyggelig afternoon was spent in the vineyard and in the rustic rural kitchen.

It had a low ceiling and flagstone floors, where we were introduced to Glennie, the lady of the house, and her son, who, by this time, was an adult. Even though I hadn't seen Glennie and her kid in a while, there was no need for formality because the atmosphere was informal and laid-back.

You can also experience a casual encounter by visiting somewhere new with close friends or family, so why not move out of your comfort zone?

Get Closer To Nature

Being in nature allows you to let your guard down and adds a certain simplicity, whether sitting by a river in Sweden, a vineyard in France, or just in your garden or a local park. When we are near nature, we are not preoccupied with amusing devices or juggling various choices.

There is only excellent company and good discussion, no excess or luxury. A quick way to Hygge is to use simple, leisurely, rustic components.

Being In The Present Moment

Being present in memorable moments has a part to play. Hygge is characterized by a significant focus on experiencing and appreciating the present moment. Every summer, my best friend, his father, and I would go sailing.

There was nowhere else we needed to be during that camping trip. We weren't connected. No telephone, No email. We could unwind and enjoy the occasion because we were surrounded by nature and terrific company.

I appreciate a few things more than being at the helm as the music blasts below deck beneath full white sails and a blue sky. The parts of these trips where we were docked in the harbors we visited were the most enjoyable. Every night after dinner, we all sat on the deck to watch the sun go down while enjoying our post-dinner Irish coffees and listening to the wind in the ship's sails. Hygge is that.

Utilizing some of the components mentioned earlier may be the best way to create hygge experiences. Occasionally, you might be able to fit every item into the pot. That occurs for me in vacation cabins. In many respects, living in a cabin gives all of the aforementioned benefits. Many of my greatest childhood leisure memories revolve around a small summer cabin we used to rent for my family every year, about six miles outside of the city from May to September.

My brother and I would relish the never-ending summer days when even the night was devoid of darkness at that time of year. We would play football, ride bicycles, explore tunnels, climb trees, catch fish, create dams and forts, sleep in tree huts, and hide under boats on the beach—all in the spirit of Hygge and leisure.

Savor And Be Grateful for The Moment

Savoring is primarily about thankfulness. It is about appreciating the present and the straightforward joys of delectable cuisine and pleasant company. It is paying proper attention to the whipped cream-topped hot chocolate. Simply put, Hygge is all about living in the present and making the most indulging in leisurely moments.

We frequently nag one another to not take anything for granted. When you get a present, saying "thank you" isn't enough to express gratitude. It involves remembering that you are living in the now, allowing yourself to appreciate your life as it is, and concentrating on all you have rather than all you lack. Clichés?

Totally. We are, unfortunately, eager to adapt to new things and events, especially pleasant ones, because our emotional system enjoys novelty. As a result, you must think of fresh reasons to express gratitude rather than letting your mind wander to the same old ideas.

Studies claim that feeling grateful encourages people to stand back and appreciate what they have more and reduces the likelihood that they will take it for granted. Because Hygge is primarily about relishing small joys, it can help us feel appreciative of the ordinary.

Hygge is maximizing the present, but it's also a strategy for preparing for and keeping enjoyment through simple leisure activities or hobbies. Because of this, Hygge might be one of the explanations for why Danes consistently report high levels of happiness. In addition to having policies that guarantee them time to explore meaningful connections.

Danes value spending time with their families and friends and cultivating lasting relationships.

Hygge During Office Hours

Hygge, however, is not just about curling up in your hyggekrog at home in front of the fire, drinking Irish coffees on the deck, or enjoying comfortable cottages. The Danish think that Hygge can— and should—occur at work. So how might office hours be made cozier or more leisurely? Well, obviously, cakes and candles.

But this is only the beginning. Consider how you can make things more informal, comfortable, and egalitarian. Here are five suggestions to encourage Hygge in the workplace.

Five simple Hyggelig activities

1. Organize A Potluck Friday: Why not plan potlucks for lunch one day a week instead of packing a lunch for yourself? Everyone feels hygge when they share.
2. Set Up An Office Garden: You can increase the Hygge by adding a few plants if the workspace or the surroundings permit it. It might be an excellent method to reduce stress by giving them a little attention each day. If you plant vegetables you can eat for lunch, you get bonus points for Hygge.

3. Bring Your Dog To Work: This is an excellent way to increase productivity by setting timed goals to give the fluffy one a much-needed belly rub for you and them.

4. Try To Make The Office More Homely: Ask your manager if they could perhaps install a few couches for individuals to use when they need to do a fast-casual meeting or have long papers to read.

5. Hygge Cubicle Life: Perhaps you are unable to alter the workplace, but what about your desk? Would it be possible to add some plants and keep some cozy socks in the drawer for working in the evenings? You might also take it a step further and envision your workspace as the Batcave of Hygge, becoming the unsung hygge hero. At the same time, your coworkers are eating lunch, the one who leaves a delicious piece of chocolate on their desks.

A Simple Leisure Itinerary From Jan To Dec

Some people believe the weather in Denmark is gloomy, windy, and damp; others claim there are two distinct winters, one gray and one green. It should be no surprise that Danes spend most of their time indoors during the winter, given the weather.

Most Danes try to spend as much time outside as they can during the summer in the vain hope of soaking up some sun, but from November to March, the weather drives Danes to stay indoors.

All Danes have left to do during the winter is hygge at home as they cannot participate in winter sports in their nation like Sweden and Norway or enjoy time outdoors like in southern Europe.

January: Movie night

A casual movie night with friends and family is the ideal way to unwind in January. Allow everyone to bring food to share, and choose an old classic you have all watched. This way, it won't matter much if folks talk a little throughout the movie. Finding the quickest method to summarize the plot of the chosen movie is a fun addition to movie night.

The Lord of the Rings trilogy and Forrest Gump became "Drug-addicted girls take advantage of a mentally handicapped boy for decades" and "Group spends nine hours returning jewelry," respectively.

February: Ski trip

Plan a trip to the mountains at this time of year with your friends and family if you have the chance. The most excellent part of the ski trip is the Hygge, despite the breathtaking mountain views, thrilling slope speeds, and incredible air quality.

The magic happens when you, your friends, and your family return to your cabin after a long day on the slopes to unwind with coffee in peace. Don't forget to bring the Grand Marnier!

March: Theme month

This could be a method to jumpstart the Hygge if you and your family are planning a summer vacation. Spend March doing a virtual tour of Spain if you're heading there. To get a head start on the language, I mean "exploring" by watching Spanish movies, cooking tapas, and, if you have kids, perhaps spending one evening writing Post-its in Spanish on the chairs (sillas), table (mesa), and plates (platos).

If you aren't going on vacation this year, you can choose your dream location or use a theme from a nation you have previously visited (get out the photo albums). Bring the country home if you can't travel there.

April: Hiking and cooking over an open fire

April may be an excellent month for those who enjoy paddling, hiking, and camping. Weather-wise, it might be a little chilly, so don't forget to carry those woolen socks (they are hot), but the month has advantages because there are fewer mosquitoes.

Without Wi-Fi, "What the hell are we going to do out here?" Your heart rate and stress levels will decrease once you get through this. Hiking is a hygge Easter egg because it promotes slowness, rusticity, and community.

The cuisine will be prepared, simmered over the fire while you gather wood for the fire, and then enjoyed with your friends while sipping whiskey outside after dinner. If you're going somewhere for Easter, don't forget to bring the chocolate eggs for the kids.

May: Weekend cabin

May is the best month to start using the countryside because the days are growing longer; meaning there's more time for leisure and hobbies. The more primitive the cabin, the more hygge; perhaps one of your friends has access to one, or you can find an inexpensive rental.

An added benefit is a fireplace. Pack some board games for gloomy days. May weekends may also offer the first chance to have a BBQ. Nothing like hanging out by the grill with a beer in your hand for summer hygge.

June: The summer solstice and elderflower cordial

Elderflowers can be harvested early June and used to make cordial or lemonade.

On June 23, St. John's Eve, Danes observe the summer solstice. My favorite custom is this one. In Denmark, the sun sets in June at 11 p.m. on a night that never truly goes dark.

As the sun starts to slowly set, there is a bittersweet recognition that the days will get shorter tomorrow, and we will begin the long ascent into darkness. This would be the perfect night for a picnic. Gather your loved ones and ignite a bonfire.

(Because of the light, they are typically lit relatively late; if you need to occupy the youngsters while you wait, this is a fantastic occasion for an egg-and-spoon race.)

Elderflower cordial

This elderflower cordial will smell of summer whether you drink it warm in the winter or cold on a hot summer day. Additionally, your home will smell like summer hygge when you make the cordial by leaving the flowers and lemons in a pan for twenty-four hours. Just one sniff instantly takes me back to the summers I spent as a child.

Ingredients

- 30 clusters of elderflowers
- 3 large lemons
- 6 glasses of water (48 oz, 1.2L)
- eight cups of sugar (1610g, 64 oz)

Instructions

1. Place the elderflower clusters in a big dish after thoroughly washing them.
2. Slice the lemons, scrub them in hot water, and then add them to the bowl's clusters.
3. Add the sugar after bringing the water to a boil.
4. Add the boiling water to the basin holding the lemon segments and elderflower clusters.
5. Place a lid on the bowl and allow the lemonade to sit for three days.
6. Pour the liquid into bottles after straining it. Put it in the refrigerator to cool down and serve when ready.

July: Summer picnic

Danes appreciate spending time outdoors in July. The evenings are still long, and the weather is warm. This time of year is ideal for a picnic in a park, on a meadow, or by the sea. Those are a few options but leave the city out. Invite your loved ones, friends, neighbors, or newcomers down the street.

Make it a potluck gathering so that everyone brings something to offer. Because they are more egalitarian, potluck dinners are typically cozier. They emphasize sharing meals as well as duties and responsibilities.

August: The perseid meteor shower

For a starry night, bring blankets. Although the light nights at this time of year may not be ideal for stargazing, the Perseid meteor

shower comes in mid-August, typically reaching its peak activity from August 11 to 13th. With Andromeda to the east and Cassiopeia to the north, keep an eye out for the Perseus constellation in the northeast.

Bring a book of Greek mythology tales for your children to read while you wait for the shooting stars if you have any. The Eta Aquarid meteor shower is possible for persons in the southern hemisphere. It typically reaches its peak in late April or early May.

September: Mushroom foraging

Although they can be found starting in late summer, mushrooms mostly appear in the autumn. The food you have grown, caught, or foraged yourself has the best flavor and a high hygge factor.

Invite loved ones along for a foraging trip in the wild. Find an expert mushroom forager and ask them to accompany you on a forage. This would be advised because eating the wrong mushrooms can be fatal. Many towns offer group excursions.

October: chestnuts

It's time for chestnuts. Take your children's chestnut-hunting and use the nuts to carve figures of animals. Buy edible chestnuts for the grownups, cut a cross in the pointy end with a knife, and roast them at 200 degrees Fahrenheit (98 degrees Celsius) for about 30 minutes, or until the skins open and the interiors are tender.

Add some butter and salt after removing the rough outer skin. Pick purchase some mandarins, roasted chestnuts, and a copy of Hemingway's A Moveable Feast if you simply want some hygge time to yourself. It takes place in Paris in the 1920s when Hemingway was a struggling author.

November: Soup cook-off

Winter is on its way. It's time to find new soup recipes and dig out the old ones. Invite loved ones and perhaps a few neighbors over for a soup competition. Everyone contributes ingredients to make a single-person soup. Prepare many small soup servings for everyone to sample, taking turns.

My go-to recipe is a pumpkin-ginger soup, which is excellent with a bit of crème fraîche. Baking some handmade bread is something extra you may do as the host. Hygge is undoubtedly present when bread is freshly prepared.

December: ÆBLESKIVER and GLØGG (Pancake Puffs)

It's hygge season right now. Candle and candy consumption is increasing, and so are BMIs. The perfect moment to make gløgg (the recipe is above), too. Invite your friends and family around for an afternoon or evening of gløgg and aebleskiver by starting well in advance by soaking those raisins in port.

Chapter 6: Comforting Recipes For Cozy Nights In

Hygge is all about having fun with the people you care about, and one of the most acceptable ways to accomplish this is to gather for a meal or tea and cake and talk about the important (and unimportant) things in life. Food hugs, and it heals. The following recipes will help provide hygge happiness right away.

You Are What You Eat

I believe Alice Waters would be hygge if Hygge were a person. She reflects many of the essential characteristics of Hygge with a relaxed, unhurried, and leisurely way of living. She also appears to appreciate the importance of excellent, hearty meals in the company of friendly people. In recent years, there has been a lot of interest in new Nordic cuisine.

Noma, which debuted in 2003 and has been named the most outstanding restaurant in the world four times since 2010, has been the center of attention. Even if a dish of live shrimp covered in ants may grab attention, it is not a typical Danish dish. An affordable version of the traditional Danish lunch dish, smorrebrod, or open-faced sandwiches on rye bread with pickled herring or leverpostej (liver paste—a spreadable concoction of baked, chopped pig's liver and lard), is served.

You must be thinking that those ants are starting to look tasty. A typical Danish cookbook with the title 50 Shades of Meat and Potatoes would be appropriate for dinner. The average Dane consumes 105 pounds of meat annually, with pork being the most popular meat in the country.

Hygge is intimately related to the high levels of meat, sweets, and coffee consumption in Denmark. Giving yourself a treat and a vacation from the rigors of healthy living are both crucial components of the hygge lifestyle. Sweets are delicious; a cake is cozily cozy; both coffee and hot chocolate are leisurely and relaxing.

Not so much with carrot sticks. The hygge ritual always includes something wicked. However, it shouldn't be something excessive or fancy. Foie gras is not cozily cozy. Yet a warming stew, more so if we all eat from the same bowl.

Hot Drinks

Eighty-six percent of Danes believe that Hygge is associated with hot drinks. The Danes' preferred hot beverage is coffee. However, they also enjoy tea, hot chocolate, and mulled wine. You probably already know how much the Danes enjoy their coffee if you're a fan of Danish TV dramas like Borgen or The Killing. There is hardly a scenario that goes by without someone getting coffee, making coffee, or asking someone else, "Coffee?" Danish people drink about 33 percent more coffee per capita than Americans.

The Danish language makes explicit the connection between coffee and Hygge. Another compound word that combines Hygge and coffee is kaffe hygge, which is widely used. "Come to kaffe hygge," together with "kaffe hygge and cake," "kaffe hygge and exercise," and "kaffe hygge and knitting."

There is kaffe Hygge everywhere. Even kaffe Hygge has a website that encourages users to "Live life today like there is no coffee tomorrow." So while you can achieve Hygge without coffee, it certainly helps. Holding a pleasant warm cup of coffee in your hands has a calming effect. Hygge can undoubtedly flourish here.

Iced Vanilla Cookies

As they bake, these delicious cookies will fill your house with the delightful scent of vanilla. They are warm, gooey, and buttery right out of the oven—the ideal melt-in-your-mouth dessert to serve visitors.

(Produces roughly 24 cookies)

Ingredients

- 9¾ oz, (275g) Unsalted butter
- 1 Teaspoon, 0.1 oz (4.9g) Vanilla extract
- 1 Medium egg, lightly beaten
- 3½ oz (100g) Superfine granulated sugar
- 3½ oz (100g) Unsalted butter

To decorate

- 2-3 Drops of food coloring (Your choice)
- 3-4 Tablespoons, 2 oz (0.05L) water
- 14 oz (400g) Powdered sugar

Method

1. Set the oven's temperature to 375°F (190°C, Gas 5).
2. In a bowl, combine the butter and sugar by beating them together.
3. Adding a bit at a time, beat in the egg and vanilla extract.
4. Add the flour and stir until a dough forms.
5. Roll the dough to a thickness of 34 inches on a work surface lightly dusted with flour (1 cm).
6. Using cookie cutters, make cookies from the dough and place them on a baking sheet prepared with parchment paper.
7. Cookies should be baked until golden brown (around 8–10 minutes).
8. Transfer to a wire rack after allowing it to harden for 5 minutes. Make the icing while the cookies are cooling.
9. As directed on the packet, sift the powdered sugar into a sizable mixing bowl and add the water, stirring until the mixture is smooth.
10. Use a knife to easily spread the icing onto the cookies and a piping bag to add decorations. Stir in the food coloring.
11. Place aside till the icing becomes solid, and serve when ready.

` Chocolate

Indulgent hot chocolate would be hygge if it were a beverage. This decadent hot chocolate recipe is like a cozy embrace in a cup. Whether on a rainy day or a cold winter afternoon, I'm sure you'll enjoy this hot chocolate as much as I do.

(Serves one)

Ingredients

- 2 Tablespoons, 1 oz (28.3g), and (180ml)/(6 oz) milk (dairy or nut)
- ½ Teaspoon, 0.08 oz (2.84g) vanilla extract
- ¼ Teaspoon, 0.04 oz (1.42g) ground cinnamon
- 1 Tablespoon, 0.5 oz (17.7g) sugar
- 1 Tablespoon, 0.05 oz (17.7g) cocoa powder

To serve (Optional)

- Cinnamon
- Marshmallows
- Cream

Method

1. Mix the cocoa powder, sugar, milk, cinnamon, and vanilla in a mug.

2. As soon as the mixture resembles a thick syrup, stir it with a fork or a little whisk.
3. Warm the remaining milk over medium heat until it starts to boil, then pour it into the mug with the chocolate syrup and thoroughly whisk.
4. Serve with a sprinkling of cinnamon and a dollop of cream or marshmallows for extra decadence.

Roasted Chestnuts

The ideal justification for spending time with your loved ones by the fire is roasting chestnuts. When cooked to perfection, their pale interiors turn nutty, creamy, and surprisingly sweet. Serve them plain or with melted butter that has been seasoned.

(Serves 4-6)

Ingredients

- 2¼ lbs (1kg) Chestnut

For the spiced butter

- Pinch of nutmeg, salt, and sugar
- 1 Cinnamon stick
- 2 oz (60g) Unsalted butter

Method

1. Achieve a temperature of 400°F (200°C, Gas 6).
2. When roasting the chestnuts, you should make a long slit or a cross in the curving shell by using a sharp knife to lay them on their flat sides. They can flee without detonating).
3. Place in a single layer, flat-side down, on a roasting pan, and bake until the skin tears apart. It should take about 30 minutes. Peel the tough skin from the chestnuts after they are cold enough to handle. Take the sweet, white kernel out of its skin and put it in your mouth.

Method to bake on the fire

1. In a cast-iron frying pan or skillet, arrange the prepared chestnuts in a single layer.
2. Place the pan in the fire's burning embers.
3. To ensure equal cooking, flip the chestnuts occasionally. Cooking them will take 5 to 10 minutes

Instructions for the spiced butter

1. Spices, salt, and sugar are added after the butter has been melted over low heat.
2. Take off the cinnamon stick after the mixture has melted, then pour it into a small bowl for dipping.

Berry Jam

Making your jam is just one example of the tiny things that make Hygge appealing. The berries are turned into jars of delicious loveliness after an hour spent stirring, bottling, and labeling in the kitchen. These jars are now ready to be spread on warm toast or scones.

Sticky and sweet, this jam will make you feel warm and satisfied inside by creating something by hand. Pick your berries for jam for the happiest Hygge!

(Produces two small jars)

Ingredients

- 17 ½ oz 9500g) Mixed seasonal berries
- 1 ½ (0.75 oz) Tablespoons of lemon juice
- 10 ½ oz (300g) Sugar

Method

1. The berries should be put in a sizable pot, slowly brought to a boil, and then simmered for five minutes.
2. After adding the sugar, stir the mixture for 10 to 15 minutes. Add the lemon juice after taking the pan off the heat.
3. Fill sterilized jars with the jam, then cover with a lid.
4. Allow to cool and set. If kept in a cool, dry pantry, the jam will last for at least a year, but once opened, it needs to be kept in the refrigerator.

Gingerbread House

Few things better capture the magic of Christmas than a gingerbread home, which is why Christmas is the peak hygge season. Even though building a gingerbread house takes time, the whole family will be engrossed for hours, and kids will enjoy using their creativity to decorate the house with snowy frosting and treats.

(Builds one house)

Ingredients

- Unsalted butter, 175 grams, or six ¼ ounces
- 7.5 ounces (200 g) smooth, light-brown sugar
- 1 ½ tbsp, 0.75 oz lemon juice, and one teaspoon, 0.1 oz (4.9g) lemon zest
- 5 ounces of liquid (150 g) molasses
- 2 Beaten eggs
- 13 ¼ ounces (375 g) simple flour
- Two teaspoons of baking powder, 28.3g (0.9 oz)
- 1 Tablespoon 17.7g (0.5 oz) ginger root
- Ground allspice, two teaspoons 10g (0.35 oz)

For The Icing

- Egg whites, six
- 3¾ pounds (1.75 kg) (1.75 kg) sprinkled with sugar powder

- Various candies for decorating, including gum drops, licorice cubes, small fruit snacks, white chocolate buttons (roof tiles), and colored sprinkles

Method

1. Cut out forms from thin cardboard to use as templates for the house's walls and roof. You'll need a triangle gable, a roof rectangle, a side wall (4.75 x 7.75 inches)(12cm x 19cm), an end wall (4.75 x 5 inches)(12cm x 12cm), and a triangular gable (4.75 x 3 x 3 inches)(12cm x 7.5cm x 7.5cm) and a roof rectangle (4.75 x 9 inches)(12cm x 23cm).
2. Tape together the 4.75-inch-long triangular gable piece's long side and one of the 4.75-inch sides of the end wall.
3. Incorporate the butter and sugar together until they are light and frothy to create the gingerbread mixture. Lemon juice, zest, and molasses should all be added. Incorporate two beaten eggs. To create a dough, sift the flour, baking powder, and spices into the mixture. The dough on parchment paper, then put it in the fridge. Six pieces of dough should be created, with two being significantly larger than the others. On a surface that has been lightly dusted with flour, roll out the four smaller pieces, and then cut out two side walls and two end walls with triangular gables (see estimated measurements above). Cut out two roof pieces from the remaining dough by rolling them out.
4. The gingerbread forms should be placed on prepared baking sheets and baked for 10 minutes at 375°F (190°C, Gas 5) or until crisp.
5. Take out of the oven and let cool for a while. Transfer to wire racks, and leave to harden overnight. You should lightly whisk two egg whites to make the icing, then gradually add one-third of the powdered sugar until the mixture is smooth and forms firm peaks. You can now start building the house. One of the side walls should be firmly pressed into the 9-inch line of icing that has been spread or piped onto the cake board to ensure that it sits upright. To give the wall additional

stability, you might need to channel a little bit more icing down either side of it. Ice the side edges of an end wall on both sides. Spread or pipe an icing line parallel to the first wall on the board, and then push the end wall firmly into the icing. To create the walls of your home, repeat this procedure with the remaining side and end walls. Before applying, let the surface harden for at least two hours.

For the roof

1. Pipe or spread a relatively thick layer of icing on top of all the walls to serve as the foundation for the roof. Then, press the roof pieces into the icing, ensuring the roof overflows the walls to form the eaves.
2. You can join the two roof parts by piping or applying some icing along the roof's crest. Leave to harden overnight.
3. You can now get started on making some frosting to beautify your home. Four egg whites are lightly whipped, then the remaining powdered sugar is added.
4. To make doors, windows, and roof tiles for the house, use icing to adhere different candies to the structure. Add icing to the roof to make snow, then top with icing sugar.

Fruit Crumble

Fruit crumble cooked from scratch is the perfect comfort food that will prevent the flu. This apple and blackberry crumble has a thick, golden oaty topping for a delicious crunch and is flavored with cinnamon. Serve it with dollops of custard or ice cream.

(Serves 4)

Ingredients

- 5 Apples, cubed after being peeled
- 150 g or 5 ¼ ounces of blackberries
- 6 Tablespoons, 85g (3 oz) soft light-brown sugar
- ½ Teaspoon 2.84g (0.05 oz) cinnamon
- Vanilla extract, 1 teaspoon 4.9g (0.1 oz)

For the topping

- 100g (3 ½ oz) of ordinary flour
- Cinnamon and two tablespoons of brown sugar
- Unsalted butter, chilled and cubed, 1 ¾ ounces (50 g).
- 4 Tablespoons, 56.7g (2 oz) of oats

Method

1. Set the oven's temperature to 350°F (180°C, Gas 4).
2. Combine the diced apples, blackberries, sugar, cinnamon, and vanilla essence in a heavy-bottomed pot.
3. Mix thoroughly, then cook for 5 minutes over medium heat.
4. Making the topping in the meantime involves combining the flour, sugar, and cinnamon in a small bowl.
5. Oats are added after the mixture has been rubbed with butter until it resembles breadcrumbs.
6. After spooning it into the ovenproof dish, place the crumble on the fruit mixture—Bake for 15 to 20 minutes, or until bubbling and brown.

Hot Spiced Fruit Punch

Hygge is all about enjoying life with the people you love, relaxing in front of a fire, and perhaps clinking glasses as they are filled with something warm and delectable. This recipe combines exotic spices with winter fruits and is like a cozy embrace in a cup.

(Serves 6-8)

Ingredients

- Orange one
- 10 Whole cloves
- Choose a variety of juices, such as orange, red grape, pineapple, apple, and cranberry, for your 5 liters (169 oz) of unsweetened fruit juice.
- 250 ml (8.4 oz) or 1 cup of water
- ¼ Teaspoon 2.84g (0.05 oz) ground cinnamon
- ¼ Teaspoon 2.84g (0.05 oz) ground nutmeg
- 1 Stick of cinnamon (plus extra to serve)
- Star anise, one (plus additional to serve)
- 1 apple
- A small amount of cranberries
- Lemon juice from one freshly squeezed lemon

Method

1. Push the cloves into the peel of one half of the orange after cutting it in half.
2. Fill a saucepan with your mixture of fruit juices totaling one liter.
3. Then use a wooden spoon to mix in the cinnamon and nutmeg powders.
4. Add the pan along with half of the orange stuffed with cloves.
5. The star anise and cinnamon stick.
6. On a stove, warm the mixture and allow it to simmer for 20 minutes.
7. Through a sieve, pour the mixture from the pan into a basin and then into a bowl.
8. In the strainer, throw out the orange and the whole spices.
9. Slice the apple and the other half of the orange. Include the slices in the bowl along with the cranberries and lemon juice.
10. Punch should be poured into a glass using a jug or a ladle. Now light the fire, take in the icy vista outside, sit back, and unwind.

Mulled Wine

It only needs a few minutes to make and is sure to warm you from the inside. This is a fantastic seasonal party drink, thanks to the intoxicating spice fragrance. This drink will help with providing an uplifting atmosphere for you and your friends/family.

(Serves 8)

Ingredients

- A bottle of red wine bottle
- 1 Quartered orange
- 2 Ounces (60 g) of brown sugar or demerara
- 1 Stick of cinnamon
- Grated nutmeg, one teaspoon 4.9g (0.1 oz)
- Fresh bay leaf, one
- Two complete cloves
- Star anise, two

To serve (Optional)

- Orange slices with cloves on them
- One stick of cinnamon
- Anise star

Method

1. You should add one-fourth of the red wine to a saucepan.
2. Add the spices, demerara, brown sugar, and orange slices after stirring.
3. Once the sugar has dissolved, boil gently.
4. Add more sugar or spices to taste after tasting for sweetness and spice.
5. The mixture should start to resemble syrup after being brought to a boil for a few minutes to allow the spices to permeate.
6. Reduce the heat to a low setting, stir in the remaining wine and star anise, and cook for a few minutes—strain into mugs or glasses that are heatproof.
7. Serve with orange slices adorned with clove, cinnamon, and star anise if you want it even hotter.

Mulled Cider

Mulled cider is the perfect beverage for gloomy days and chilly nights spent by the fire. It not only makes your kitchen smell like a candle shop, but it also makes you feel better. Impossible to resist with its citrus, rum, clove, and apple flavors, this cider recipe is a perfect way to use up windfall apples.

(Serves 8)

Ingredients

- 8 cups (2 liters) (67 oz) cider
- Two apples studded with cloves
- Four cinnamon sticks
- Five whole allspice berries
- Zest of 1 orange
- Two measures of rum (dark is best)

To serve (Optional)

- Star anise
- Slices of apples
- Cinnamon sticks

Method

1. In a large saucepan, incorporate all the ingredients and heat to a gentle simmer for 30 minutes.
2. Take care to ensure that it does not boil.
3. Turn off the heat, strain, and pour into heatproof glasses or mugs after moving the liquid to a heatproof basin.
4. Serve with cinnamon sticks, star anise, and apple slices.

Butternut Squash Soup

Make a hearty cup of creamy butternut squash soup to welcome yourself home. This dinnertime delicacy is the nutritional equivalent of a comfortable knit sweater and is simple to make (plus, you can reheat it for lunch!).

(Serves 2)

Ingredients

- 2 Tiny or one large butternut squash
- A few freshly-chopped, fresh sage leaves
- Black pepper freshly ground
- 1 to 2 Tablespoons (14.3g/28.3g)(0.5 oz/1 oz) of olive oil
- 2 Chopped onions
- 1(1 liter)(34 oz) of vegetable or chicken stock

To serve (Optional)

- Crème fraîche
- Pumpkin seeds
- Fresh thyme leaves sprinkled on top
- Blue cheese fragment
- Both salt and pepper

Method

1. Set the oven's temperature to 350°F (180°C, Gas 4).
2. Remove the seeds from the butternut squash without peeling it, then cut it into big pieces. Combine with the black pepper, olive oil, and sage leaves. Put the mixture in a roasting pan and cook it for 35 to 45 minutes.
3. In a sizable pot, saute the onions until they are transparent while the squash is cooking. Add the mixture to the onions and cover with stock once the butternut squash has softened and the sage leaves have become crunchy. After 30 minutes of simmering, remove the pot from the heat, season to taste, and blend until smooth with a hand blender (blend for a wonderfully silky soup).
4. Decorate crème fraîche swirls and a sliver of blue cheese with fresh thyme leaves and pumpkin seeds.
5. To taste, add salt and pepper.
6. Serving suggestion: crusty bread

Popcorn

Nothing tastes better when you want to relax on the couch and watch a movie than popcorn, whether sweet or savory. This is a lovely snack for you and the whole family.

(4 Servings)

Ingredients

- 1 Tablespoon 14.3g (0.5 oz) vegetable or sunflower oil
- 50g or 1 ¾ Ounces of popping corn

To serve

- Honey
- Salt
- Butter
- Chocolate
- Powdered sugar

Method

1. Add the oil and the kernels to a sizable, heavy-bottomed pan with a tight-fitting lid. (Using a pan with a heavy base will prevent the kernels from burning during cooking.) Only add ¼ of the recommended amount of corn kernels to the pan to allow for expansion.

2. Cook the kernels in their skins until they begin to "pop" and burst out of the pan while keeping the lid on and sometimes shaking it over medium heat.
3. Take the pan off the stove, ensuring that the popping has stopped, then transfer the contents into a big bowl.
4. Sprinkle some powdered sugar, honey, or salt on the popcorn while it's still heated.
5. You could add a little to the skillet as the butter melts and swirl it into the popcorn. Pour melted chocolate over the popcorn and let it set for a special treat.

Chocolate Fondue

Chocolate fondue is a favorite of all. This simple dessert is the ideal justification for getting everyone together for an enjoyable, social evening. Fresh banana, pineapple, and strawberry chunks form delectable dunks for the decadent, creamy sauce. This rich chocolate fondue will wow your guests, whether you're entertaining friends or hosting a quiet dinner for two.

(4 Servings)

Ingredients

- 3 ¾ Cups or 110 g of sugar
- (110 ml)(3.7 oz) of Water

- 14 Ounces (400 g) chocolate (dark, milk, or white)

To serve

- Grapes
- Pineapples
- Strawberries
- Marshmallows
- Bananas

Method

1. In a medium-sized saucepan, warm the water and sugar slowly until the sugar dissolves and a syrup forms.
2. In a heatproof bowl, add the chocolate and break it into pieces. Set the bowl over a pan of simmering water. (Avoid letting the bowl's base touch the water; doing so could cause the chocolate to seize and become lumpy.)
3. To create a smooth sauce, combine the chocolate with the syrup and whisk with a wooden spoon.
4. Ensure that the sauce cools down a little before serving because it will be extremely spicy. You can serve bite-sized pieces of fresh fruit or marshmallows by dipping them in the sauce.
5. A teaspoon of peppermint essence, some orange zest, the contents of a vanilla bean, or a tablespoon of Irish cream liqueur are a few other flavorings you can use in the sauce.

Spiced Banana Bread

Spiced banana bread with a pat of fresh butter is like manna from heaven and is a tasty treat for breakfast, afternoon tea, or dessert. This moist banana bread will be an excellent treat over Christmas and Easter.

(12–15 slices per batch)

Ingredients

- 55g of Unsalted butter, or 2 ounces.
- 200g (7 oz) of Brown sugar
- 1 Beaten egg
- 3 Mashed, overripe bananas, 82.3 ounces (250 g) self-raising flour
- 1 Salt shaker
- 2 Teaspoons (28.3g) (0.9 oz) of spices (a pinch of nutmeg and cinnamon)
- Grated 1 ¾ ounces (50 g) of dark chocolate

To serve (Optional)

- Butter
- Slices of banana

Method

1. Set the oven's temperature to 350°F (180°C, Gas 4).

2. A 7.75 x 4 inch (19cm x 10cm) loaf pan should be greased or lined with parchment paper.
3. Use a wooden spoon or an electric whisk to combine the butter and sugar.
4. Add the mashed bananas and the beaten egg to the mixture.
5. Fold the flour, salt, spices, and grated dark chocolate using a spatula or wooden spoon.
6. After putting the ingredients in the loaf pan, bake it for an hour.
7. Place parchment paper on the top until the bread is done baking to prevent burning if the top appears too brown while baking.
8. Serve with butter, banana slices, or whatever else you choose!

Slow Foods Chubby Cousin

Therefore, sweets, pastries, and cakes are hyggelige. Hygge eating, though, is much more than just packing on muscle. Perhaps Hygge is leisure food. Hygge food is, however, also predominantly slow food. The way a dish is prepared can also affect how cozy it is. The general rule is that a meal is cozier the longer it cooks.

Hygge meal preparation is about taking pleasure in the systematic process of it, appreciating the time you spend, and the satisfaction of creating something worthwhile. It has to do with how you feel about the meal. Because of this, homemade jams are hyggeliger than store-bought jams.

Every morsel will transport you back to the summer day you harvested the fruit, and the strawberry aroma filled the house. I like to spend most of a Sunday afternoon cooking anything that has to bake or simmer for hours, especially in the winter. Moreover, You can add time to the process by going to a fantastic farmers' market.

In doing so, you can carefully choose the seasonal vegetables or consult with the butcher about the best meat for a stew that is simmered. Not only is it the sound of Hygge, but it also captures the spirit of Hygge to have a pot simmering on the stove while you read a book in your hyggekrog.

The only reason to stand up is to top up the stew with a little more red wine. It is crucial to emphasize that the process need not concentrate around cooking some hearty traditional Nordic food. The process, not the result, is what matters. I attempted to make limoncello last summer.

For the alcohol to absorb the flavor and color of the peel, you must soak the peels of numerous lemons in alcohol for more than a week as part of the procedure. I would open the fridge after work every day and take a thorough smell to check on the development of my mixture. The outcome was mediocre, but the experience of watching the bottle's development in the refrigerator was thoroughly hygge, and I may have discovered a new hobby along the way.

Chapter 7: The 5 Dimensions Of Hygge

Hygge is an attitude. Sometimes I worry that we might forget that in the deluge of social media updates and brilliantly styled Instagram photos. It is a manner of being and taking in the world. Being more aware of the present moment is a terrific method to connect with these feelings.

Each of us has a distinct method for doing this, whether it involves photography, meditation, cooking, drawing, or some other leisure or hobby activity. There is no need to go out and buy an expensive throw to start enjoying the hygge lifestyle; instead, activities that make us stop and think about what we are doing and what is around us are a terrific way to get started!

The Taste Of Hygge

Because hygge frequently involves eating, the taste is a crucial component. And it can't be overly novel, unconventional, or complex. Hygge almost always has a familiar, sweet, and cozy flavor. Adding honey to tea makes it cozier and more hyggelig. You can apply icing to a cake to make it more relaxed. Additionally, you can add wine to your stew to make it more hyggelig.

The Sound Of Hygge

The most pleasing sounds are perhaps the tiny sparks and quick crackles of burning wood. But if you live in an apartment and can't have an open fire without running a significant danger of death, don't panic. Many noises have hyggelig qualities.

In reality, Hygge is primarily characterized by the lack of noise, which allows you to hear even incredibly soft noises like rain on the roof, the wind blowing outside the window, the sound of trees swaying in the wind, or the creaks of wooden planks that flex under your feet.

Hyggelig sounds can also include someone cooking, knitting, or painting. Hygge's soundtrack will consist of any sound that conjures up a secure feeling. For instance, if you are indoors and feel secure, the sound of thunder can be quite hyggeligt; if you are outside, not so much.

Smells Like Hygge

Have you ever experienced a scent that transports you to a period of time or location where you felt secure? Or experienced a smell that, more than a recollection, brought back memories of how the world appeared to you as a child?

Another possibility is that certain smells elicit strong sentiments of safety and comfort, such as the smell of a bakery, the aroma of the apple trees in your childhood yard, or perhaps the comforting aroma of your parents' home.

People's perceptions of what makes a smell hyggelig vary greatly since smells link current situations to those that they have previously associated with that smell. The scent of cigarettes in the morning can either make you feel sick or give you a headache, depending on who you ask.

All of the hygge-inspired scents have one thing in common: they serve as a reminder of security and nurturing. We use smell to sense whether something is safe to eat, but we also use it to intuit whether a place is safe and how alert we should be.

The smell of Hygge is the smell that tells you to put your guard down completely. The smell of cooking, the smell of a blanket you use at home, or the smell of a place we perceive as safe can be very hyggeligt because it reminds us of a state of mind we experienced when we felt completely safe.

What Does Hygge Feel Like?

As I indicated, Hygge can be evoked by letting your fingers glide over a wooden surface, around a warm porcelain cup, or through the hairs on a reindeer's skin. Old, labor-intensive handcrafted goods always have a higher degree of coziness than newly produced goods.

And little things are always cozier than larger ones. Denmark's motto is "The smaller, the more hyggeligt," as opposed to the United States "The bigger, the better." Nearly all of the buildings in Copenhagen are merely three or four stories tall.

The hygge factor in these historic structures is more substantial than that in new homes composed of steel, glass, and concrete. Anything made by hand, including items made of wood, ceramics, wool, leather, and other materials, is considered hyggeligt. Although they can be if they are old enough, shiny metal and glass are not hyggeligt.

The hygge touch is attracted to the organic, rustic surface of things that are flawed or have been or will be impacted by aging. In addition, being warm is not the same as feeling warm while inside something warm in a chilly environment. It creates the impression that you are at ease in a hostile setting.

Seeing Hygge

As we've already mentioned, Hygge is very much about light. Too much brightness is not cozy. Hygge, however, also emphasizes taking your time. You can note this by observing languid motions, such as the lazily flickering flames of an open fire, gently falling snow, or aqilokoq, as the Inuits would say.

In summary, hyggelige is defined as slow, organic movements and dark, natural colors. It is not the sight of a clean, well-lit hospital or the presence of moving traffic. Slow, rustic, and dim is hygge.

The Sixth Sense Of Hygge

The concept of Hygge is safety. Therefore, Hygge is a sign of confidence in your surroundings and the people you are with. And the hygge sensation is a sign that you feel happy when someone advises you to follow your gut instinct, that you have opened up your comfort zone to include other people, and that you feel like you can be wholly authentic with other people.

Hygge can be felt, heard, tasted, smelled, touched, and seen. However, Hygge is most notably felt. Winnie-the-Pooh was referenced at the beginning of the book, and I believe his advice is still valid today. You don't spell love. It's palpable. This brings us to the book's final subject, which is joy.

Addicted To Hygge

While you can purchase a cake, happiness cannot, at least in our brain's judgment, be bought. Open a coffee shop's door in your mind. As soon as you enter, the welcoming fragrances from everything on the counter tempt you, and when you see all the pastries and cakes, you feel delighted.

Your body starts to feel euphoric as you take the first piece of your favorite cake, which you have chosen. Yes, that is a good thing. But have you thought about why consuming sugary foods makes you so happy? There is a structure called the nucleus accumbens in the basal forebrain.

It is a component of the brain's reward system and plays a big part in reinforcement, motivation, and pleasure. Like all vertebrates, we have this system because we must enjoy activities like eating and having sex. After all, they're essential to the survival of our species.

A chemical is released in the brain, and the signaling chemical dopamine is triggered when you are engaged in an activity that is seen as gratifying. Dopamine is released in reward circumstances from a region of the brain called the ventral tegmental area, which is close to the nucleus accumbens.

We feel pleasure when dopamine is transported from nerve fibers to receptors in various areas of the brain. The cerebral cortex stores pleasant event memories so we won't forget them. Although it may sound bizarre, you could claim that the brain develops addictions for us to survive.

Sweet breast milk is the first thing we taste when we are born. Our preference for sweet foods is necessary for survival, which explains why we feel happy when we consume cakes and other sweet treats and struggle to quit. Our bodies have taught us to carry on with actions that result in rewards.

When it comes to fat and salt, the same principle applies. In other words, we link a particular food with pleasure, which makes us need more of it. If you want to eat cake, have some cake. Hygge is something that is meant to be and feel pleasant for you. However, we also need to know when to stop.

Conclusion

Find leisure in your life through Hygge hobbies

We strive to comprehend what motivates eudaemonia, affective or hedonic enjoyment, and life satisfaction. Of course, there are connections among the many dimensions. You are more likely to report higher levels of life satisfaction if your daily experiences are good.

The second dimension, however, is far more unstable. Here, we can see the weekend influence. People report feeling happier on weekends than on weekdays due to having time to indulge in leisure and hobby activities. Most people wouldn't be surprised by this because on weekends; we are more inclined to engage in things that make us feel good.

Furthermore, there is a biological connection between the many aspects of happiness and how you spend your free time. Many of the brain systems involved in the hedonic experience of sensory pleasure are also engaged in the higher eudaemonic expertise. There is a correlation between hedonic and eudaimonic well-being.

When embracing Hygge, I believe that one of the most intriguing discoveries in recent years is that good emotions matter more to our general well-being than negative ones regarding our lifestyle and overall life satisfaction. Through my research and writing for this book, I've learned that Hygge might act as a constant source of happiness through sharing experiences, enjoying some leisure or downtime, or simply partaking or sharing in hobbies.

Hygge provides us with the language, the goal, and the strategies for preparing for and maintaining happiness—and obtaining a small amount of it each day. When we go home from a long work day on a chilly, rainy January day, Hygge may be the closest thing we have to bliss. And let's face it, most of our lives will be lived this way— Daily, not only on chilly January days.

We might find ourselves on a beach in an exotic location once a year, or more if we're lucky, and we might discover Hygge and happiness there. Hygge focuses on maximizing what we already have in abundance: the ordinary hobbies and leisure activities we conduct throughout our lifestyles. So why not leap out of your comfort zone and try an exciting new hobby to shed some joy on your Hygge lifestyle and embrace Hygge living?

Printed in Great Britain
by Amazon

43156145R00059